Sun kissed: Poetic Verses of Resilience and Grace

Nicolett Charles

BookLeaf Publishing

India | USA | UK

Presentation by *BookLeaf Publishing*

Web: www.bookleafpub.com

E-mail: info@bookleafpub.com

ISBN:9789358317503

First edition 2024

DEDICATION

To the resilient spirits who refuse to be defined by the shadows of their past, this collection of verses is dedicated.

For every soul navigating the labyrinthine paths of life, finding solace in the embrace of words, these poems are offered as a beacon of hope.

To the little people whose voices often fade into the background, may these verses echo your stories and aspirations, reminding the world of your worth and strength.

In memory of the moments that shaped me and the people who inspired me, this anthology stands as a tribute to the human spirit's unwavering tenacity and capacity for boundless compassion.

ACKNOWLEDGEMENT

In the quiet recesses of my heart, I extend my deepest gratitude to all those who have woven threads of inspiration, support, and understanding into the tapestry of my life, shaping this collection of verses. To my family, who have been the sturdy pillars of my existence, your love and unwavering belief have fueled my journey, infusing these poems with the essence of our shared experiences.

I am indebted to the serendipitous encounters and the friendships forged along winding paths, each soul leaving an indelible mark on my narrative. To the mentors and guides who illuminated my path with wisdom and patience, your influence resonates within these verses, guiding my pen as it dances across the page.

To my children, who have been both my muse and my motivation, your innocence and resilience have been a source of boundless inspiration, infusing these poems with a mother's tender affection and fierce determination.

Lastly, to every reader who embarks on this poetic odyssey, your willingness to traverse the

landscapes of my soul is a gift beyond measure.
May these words resonate within your heart,
whispering tales that resonate with your own
experiences and emotions.

With heartfelt appreciation,
Nicolett Charles

PREFACE

Within these pages lie the echoes of moments, each caught in the delicate web of time, woven intricately to express the myriad emotions and thoughts that have painted the canvas of my life. This collection of poems is a memoir, not in the traditional sense of prose and chapters, but in the lyrical cadence of verses that mirror my journey. Every stanza holds a fragment of my existence, a snippet of joy, sorrow, hope, and resilience that have been the threads weaving through the fabric of my days. Through these verses, I offer a glimpse into the tapestry of my soul, inviting you to traverse the corridors of my experiences, to feel the resonance of emotions etched in ink—a symphony of moments whispered, shouted, and softly spoken, encapsulating the essence of my being. This anthology stands as a testament to the power of words, how they become vessels for healing, understanding, and connection, transcending time and space to touch the hearts of kindred spirits.

Cry Baby Cry

Cry baby Cry

My eyes see you in a light no one else has,

Your deep voice of Love echoes to my heart.

The soft care you made me feel was so
comforting, until I fell asleep in your arms.

 Your laughter was filled with the motivation of
wanting me to succeed.

The sweet Awes that pressed through your heart
filled with love wanting me to stay this size
forever.

Cry baby Cry

My heart seeing the longing in your eyes when
you had to drive away, leaving your children to
fate

Racing heart cries as you know it will be a long time before we meet again

Crying myself to self to sleep only to wake up and realize you are still gone

Days seem like months, standing in the doorway waiting for you to return

Deep down inside I can't feel our connection anymore

Tears rolling down my face as I try to adapt to the newfound home I was forced to live

The Sun will shine again.

Cry baby Cry

Living out of a bag

I hated moving,

We moved a lot as kids and I never felt safe
enough to relax not knowing when
we will have to grab all we can hold and go.

The shame of all our things being put to the
street as we exit the school bus, not
understanding why

Seeing this one man possess them all, the houses
we call home and if he didn't have his way we
lose everything we own.

He held a shrewd smile as we see him leave my
moms room

His pale skin made me uneasy not knowing
whats to come

New house more rooms to clean and less things
so fill them with

Echoes as we play , one dresser , one bed, one
sheet and very few clothes

The one sheet we use to sleep , was held close to
keep warmth from leaving the room

Fight to understanding the basic needs to survive
on our own for days

Scared for anyone to knock on the door to tell
us to leave

Dreaming of a permit home with a yard filled of
fruit trees

Lights and water being disconnected

Implementing the survival plan we were taught
as soon as we could walk.

Fifth or Twenty fifth home ,does it matter ,
whose counting

There is never a number that can hold

Neighbors come and go no matter the
connection or Love

When will this end

I hate moving.

From the Country to City

Growing up in a small town where everyone
knows everyone
From only one school for each grade to the
candy house on the corner
From Bluebirds to Robert Food Mart
The Fresh linen on the clothing line to the
crickets playing in the Bayou
The popcorn smell when the Fair comes to town
to the Fourth of July fireworks at the City Hall
The safeness you feel due to everyone knowing
each other or knowing their families.
 It was moving day and all has changed
Animals in fields I never seen before and hurds
of cars moving in one direction
A new life I was unaware of the dramatic change
that is about to take place
Arriving to my new home to hear the hustle and
bustle of the city
Ambulance sirens are loud and alarming
Dogs barking uncontrollably was new ,but
familiar
So many schools to chose from and friends to
make
The different types of food and the different
type of ways to prepare them

Neighbors that don't speak
But the need to mind your own business was a
rule
No clothes on the lines unless you are
underprivileged
No "yes ma'am" or No "yes Sir" needed (it was
frowned upon)
But The freedom the city life gives is
unrelenting
The way the fast pace living gives you the
adrenaline you need to motivate yourself to do
more
The unlimited options was a wave of optimism
The change was harsh but necessary
The city became my newfound love
I cant go back to what I know this can't be
unseen
One things for sure
I am in love with this city

Being a Mom

Being young mother was not my ideal chose of
beginning this journey

You came too swift and unexpected I was not
ready to love you but it was there

You grew to what seems so fast

Not knowing where we would live or go but ,I
know I was you mom

To feel you move so soft and noticeable at times
made me wonder how you look
and what you will be come

You changed my life forever you won

All my choses is no longer my own ,I never be
alone

Everything I thought I wanted has changed

You are my only priority, Nothing else in the
world matter

We are life partners forever

We will grow together through each faze our
lives and try to beat this thing called life .

I love you

12th Birthday

I was do excited my own birthday, sharing one with my sibling of 11 months 3 weeks and 4 days was great but not individually fulling

The sound of the music playing and adults laughing ,family cursing at each other made me feel safe

Trying to take to take in every moment that was given to me was overwhelming

Playing tag was extra special ,this time around

The warm sun kissing my cheek goodnight

Al Green blaring through the speakers as they call for us to come eat

Crickets sing and lightning bugs soaring in the dust ski

Dominions and cards keeping the adults at bay, children's laughter and screaming at each other

The street light didn't matter today, all the adults
was out to play

Cigarettes and Alcohol was always apart of the
game

Oh no someone breaks out in dance and to
"Down home Blues by Z.Z Hill "

 The "O's" and "Get it girl" caught my eye

To turn and fixated on to Frankie Rhone singing
in to the night

Tired and ready to chase Mr. Sandman

I find my way back to my room and soon the Tv
was watching me .

It was one of the best days of my life

Life is Love

Life is love
Life is a gift that can be taken away
Life is a present that you continuously unwrap
Life is a treasure that everyone seek to find
Life is a river that only flow one way
Life is a road that you can only travel once
You only get one , how are you treating it?

Stress

Thought that run free in our heads due to Stress

" School - I have to complete to provide "

"Work - Task that need to be completed in order to look good to get that promotion."

" Home - Clean - clean and maintain "

"Religion - Study the word and try to be a good person "

"Family - Call more, try to spend time "

"Finances- Make more money, and pay the bills"

"Relationship - Love them , fill their cup ,continue to grow "

The stress of life and how we deal with them matters.

It may sound like a lie but the answer is "One day at a time "

Company

To sit with you calms me, to watch a movie or
listen to the traffic that flow is all that I now
know

Our patio is place of peace, we laughed and we
cried

Relive our past and profound moments where
we see our past in a new way

To take control of the healing process

All the flowers and wine has way of relaxing our
mind

Allowing you to process all the pain and use it
as fuel to start on journey through our past lives
to heal and move forward.

When the doors swing open we let the healing
began .

Aware

Being aware of death is a gift that steals
moments from you that is never given back .
The constant worry and living with constant
concern, stealing all the present moments like a
thief in the night.
You won't be aware until the memories began to
fleets you as a bird flying away for migration
Confused on what is happening in front of you is
debilitating .
Trying to convince your family you are ok .
Mediation and holistic herbs help to calm you,
Music and prayer to comfort you
Being told one day it will not be ok .
I am very aware

Grandmother

   A grandmother is love wrapped up in a
mother's love.
You feel the connection to a living being you
didn't birth but is willing to die for
To protect and love no matter what
A connection to your child that you gave life to.
The desire for you to succeed and pass on the
legacy to be remembered for years to come .
To be the ancestor after my passing
To love you unconditionally and your parents
not object
Go ahead lil one grow to be you .
Grandmother will be here waiting .

Sleepless Nights

Sleep that escapes me
Nights that have you lying awake wanting to
find and chase down the rest your mind seeks.
Eyes closed no rest Around
Sleep escapes you is profound
Heart yearn for rest eyes closed
God sees it ,God hears it ,God knows
May your nights be filled with rest and comfort
to sooth your soul
Sleep that escapes you
Your mind can't rest due to all the stress and it
won't let you express the lack of mind control
you have due to the rest that fleets you
Sleep that escapes you

We all going to die

We all are going to die
When ,where , how we don't know.
But positively going to happen
Some will be diagnosed with a terminal illness
or disease towards to given a time to aim to
guide them to get their affairs in order
We all are going to die
Some will not make it home from a trip to the
store ,school , church or work .
Some may have been blessed to have lived a
long life and their time is up but
We all are going to die
Hopefully you understand that it is the end we
all get one and its something we can not stop
Some deaths are planned so there is no surprise,
many feel this is a unwise and selfish method.
But everyone is not built to face it
Some get more time than others that is the
problem and its out of our control
We all are going to die
Lets try to make everyday count no matter the
method or the reason.
 Death ends all seasons, like I stated
We all are going to die

First Love

He smiles at me with this short but strong smile
He knows to be the strongest of the group,
attraction
The way he smells is undeniable attractive
The feel of his rough hands as he rubs my face
to comfort me
The way he text and call to check on me to
reassure his heart I am safe
The way he put me first in any given moment it
is needed willing to go to war for love
Things are funnier when we are lost in each
other eyes
Having every waking moment with him is
necessary
All of the stuffed animals, necklaces, rings and
perfumes piles grow with the smalls affirmations
that are given
Finding little notes that gives me an
unintentional smile as I read your heart on paper.

This love is unknown this love is new .

Daughter

I heard the news I was having a girl and my
heart fluttered with excitement
To know we will dress alike and maybe grow
close is a blessing
To love a girl with the depth of my heart closer
than my sister and my friend
Sharing food and baths for 9 mths was great but
to know you are on your way to meeting me
for the first time put me in a new state
Baby cried out loud and my heart stop for a
second , head full of hair and the most beautiful
eyes
My babygirl has made her entrance, I am so
proud
One day we be so connected that our souls
would be merged in Love .
I love you babygirl

DAD

You left me too soon and left an open wound
I cried myself to sleep to mask the pain ,I felt
like a baby crying in the rain
My love never known a bound I cant wait to see
u again but until that time
I will hold on to the memories that I found
You are apart of my heart and with that we can
never part
Please believe I am still your little girl and you
was always my world.

Sister Sight

Hello Sisters I am here with you
We was born together and the bond can not be
broken
We learn to walk and talk together
We began school together and protected one
another
At times I was the oldest and you were the
youngest
but either way you are my sisters
I've been through heart aches and pains with
you and your love have no bound
We will be there for wedding, funerals , births
and teen pains ,
I am here for the long ride and to keep you sane
You are my sister and our love will be forever
Love you babygirl

Sun

Sun is beautiful
The sun is everything we need
It helps to make us feel better
To caress the Melanin in our skin
The Sun is a Goddess that will always win

One

One love
One life
One mind
One heart
One Step
All it takes is One

Family Love

In a tranquil realm where dreams take flight,
A village of kin, bathed in golden light.
Families intertwined, hearts beating as one,
Underneath the arch of the warming sun.

Houses adorned with laughter's embrace,
Love woven into every dwelling place.
Each window tells tales of joy and care,
A mosaic of bonds, beyond compare.

In this hamlet, each soul finds its space,
Nurtured by kin, in an endless embrace.
Children dance freely, their laughter a song,
Elders share wisdom, lifelong and strong.

Through trials and triumphs, they stand as a
whole,
United in spirit, an unbroken soul.
Shouldered burdens become lighter to bear,
With love and support, always there.

Hands join in to build and create,
A haven of solace, an eternal estate.
With each sunrise, a new chapter begins,
In this village of kin, where love always wins.

User
Family love
ChatGPT
Family love, an endless sea,
Binding hearts in harmony.
A gentle embrace, a guiding light,
Through darkest hours and brightest sight.

It's in the whispers, soft and kind,
A sheltering haven, a peace of mind.
In laughter's echo, joy takes flight,
Mending wounds with pure delight.

Shared stories weave a timeless thread,
Memories cherished, never to shred.
Through highs and lows, a steadfast shore,
Love's embrace, an endless store.

In trials faced and battles won,
Family love stands, second to none.
A tapestry woven, strong and true,
Binding souls, old and new.

It's the warmth in a glance, a hand to hold,
A treasure trove, more precious than gold.

Family love, an eternal flame,
Forever burning, in each other's name.

Divorce

Divorce with pain, a bitter tide,
Shattering dreams where love once thrived.
A rift that tears through hearts in two,
Leaving scars, both old and new.

The echoes of vows, once sweetly spoken,
Now drowned in tears, hearts left broken.
Fragments of a life, scattered, untamed,
In the aftermath of a love unclaimed.

It's the silent cries in the dead of night,
The ache that lingers, a relentless fight.
Promises shattered, hopes turned to dust,
In the unraveling of a bond, once robust.

Children caught amidst the storm,
Their innocence bruised, a heavy swarm.
Navigating worlds now torn apart,
Searching for solace, a brand-new start.

Yet, from this pain, may resilience rise,
A phoenix from ashes, towards the skies.
Healing begins, slow and frail,
As hearts find strength to set sail.

For in endings, seeds of new beginnings sow,
A chance to grow, to thrive, to glow.
Divorce with pain, a chapter's close,
But in healing, new possibilities pose.

Phoenix

In the midst of turmoil, a spirit refined,
A resilient soul, unyielding, defined.
Through trials and storms, you endure,
A beacon of strength, resolute and sure.

Scars adorned like badges of might,
Each one a story of a valiant fight.
In the face of adversity, you stand tall,
A testament to perseverance overall.

You've weathered storms, faced the dark,
Yet your flame burns bright, an eternal spark.
A survivor, forged in life's fiery trial,
Your spirit unbroken, your heart worthwhile.

Strength isn't absence of pain or despair,
But the courage to rise, to boldly declare:
"I am a warrior, a victor in my own right,
I'll navigate through the darkest night."

Your resilience, a symphony of grace,
A testament to the human race.
Strong survivor, your journey's not done,
Your resilience shines; you've already won.

www.ingramcontent.com/pod-product-compliance
Lightning Source LLC
La Vergne TN
LVHW010942200726
843509LV00013B/2269